BRAVE

and

FREE

Dedication

This book is dedicated to the people who gave their lives to protect this land and to those who are currently serving our country. We owe them all our deepest gratitude for their sacrifice so we may live in this land of the "brave and free".

Brian,
Thank you for your service to our country so we may all live in the land of the "Brave and free"

Sue Mc Collum

First Edition

Other books by Sue McCollum
Moving On (before and after cancer)

Published by
Blue Dot Publishing
bluedotpublishing@yahoo.com

ISBN 0-9722313-1-5

Printed by
Prodigy Press, Inc.
Menlo Park, CA

Acknowledgments

This book was written at a time in history when our nation was in shock and disbelief. We were reeling from the outrageous and evil events of 9-11 and were looking for leaders - and heroes. Fortunately, we found both.

Three firefighters, George Johnson, Dan McWilliams and Bill Eisengrein, were captured in a photo by Thomas E. Franklin, a staff reporter for The Record (Bergen County, NJ) standing in the midst of rubble and debris but representing the undaunted spirit, hope, and bravery of the people of the U.S.A.

The Bravest Fund, (www.thebravestfund.com) was started by these three firefighters to benefit the firefighters, police officers, other rescue personnel, and their families. All proceeds from this book, Brave and Free, will be given to this fund.

I would like to thank The Record (www.northjersey.com) for allowing me to use a sketch of this copyrighted photograph. This sketch, by Greg Ocasek of Aki Designs, was chosen to remind us of the courage and bravery of the men and women in the U.S.A. today.

Pastor David Moore also provided strong leadership to a country awash in sorrow, grief, and fear. Two poems, Grief and Our Response, were inspired by his teaching and I thank him for providing the inspiration and material for these two poems.

I would be amiss if I did not acknowledge that this book required love, care, and the prayers of many. Each has helped, in their own way, to write this book and I thank them for their support. Ed Greene, John Jenks, Kathy Noverr, Jean Dawes, Mary Lou McCollum, Terri Miller, Ellie Nelson, Helen Carter, Rita Mungioli, Greg Ocasek and to my husband, Bob, who has lived each page with me.

Introduction

The events of September 11th have stirred my emotions, heart, and soul. As a poet, my pen has turned patriotic and I am writing about our great nation, our faith, our friends, our family, and those who make sacrifices for this wonderful country in which we live.

These poems are a poet's view of these past few weeks - what has happened and the lives that have been altered by this event forever.

May God Bless You
and
God Bless America!

October, 2001

Table of Contents

Shock!

America Fights Back

The People

Standing Up

Shock!

Unbelievable!

How could this ever happen
in the good old U.S.A?
The World Trade Center, in New York City,
was demolished - yesterday.

The whole world watched this horrible sight
it was unbelievable to see -
Our own plane flew into the Center
while thousands tried to flee.

Full of fuel, the explosion was mighty
the hole in the building was large.
The plane disappeared in a cloud of smoke -
it looked like a dynamite charge.

First one tower, then the other -
came tumbling to the ground.
Thousands of people lost their lives
in this enormous, cement mound.

To kill so many people
in such a calculated way -
Only shows the depth of evil
that live in some men - today.

But good will conquer evil
it always has - and always will.
The U.S.A. will survive...
a country with a strong will.

9-12-01

The Best of the Best

The best of the best is gone;
blown away in a useless attack.
They were the cream of the crop -
and in intelligence they did not lack.

They went to work and were doing their job
as all good Americans do;
When an unprovoked attack occurred
of which they had - no clue.

Instantly killed, blown away,
with this horrific, terrorist attack.
It came so fast many did not
even have time to react.

The husbands and wives, daughters and sons,
all gone in a blink of an eye.
America will never be the same -
it is hard to say, "Good-bye."

9-13-01

Get Out!

Etched into our mind forever
is the World Trade Center crash.
A plane crashing into the tower
in the center of this steel mass.

An explosion and a fire ball
we were then able to see.
Unbelievable is what it was
shocking the world - and me.

This is war! You've made your point,
killing thousands of innocent people.
The Holocaust - again we relive
gone - thousands of wonderful people.

Get out! Go home! We don't need you here
enjoying the freedoms of life.
You take the 'good' that's offered here
then cause our nation strife.

So long, good bye, go back to your home.
Don't exploit us any longer.
This nation is the greatest in the world
and we will indeed grow stronger.

Good and evil are always at war.
We've walked this path before.
We know who we are and what we're about
- and it's not about killing and gore.

This is America - where freedom prevails.
You must love what America stands for.
It's time to separate the good from the bad
and kick the terrorists out the door.

9-13-01

God and Country

The World Trade Center came crashing down
for the entire world to see.
But the foundation is still there
strong as it can be.

So too with the American people.
The foundation is still strong.
What was done to the World Trade Center
was horrific and terribly wrong.

But this cowardly act has only
united this great nation of ours.
Many of our average people
now stand as shining stars.

They've stepped up to the plate to help
rescue their fellow man.
They've risked their lives over and over
doing all that they can.

It's a fight between good and evil
and the freedoms of this great land.
We are a strong and mighty nation
built on rock - not sinking sand.

We will survive this horrific ordeal
and we'll ask our God to bless;
Our great nation and its' people
we will, in Him, find rest.

9-15-01

It's Over

We have now experienced evil.
It was here and very clear.
Killing and destroying thousands -
filling people with great fear.

We have never known such terror
in this great land of ours,
We have lulled ourselves into sleep
worshipping the wrong stars.

Now that this has happened
a new 'Star' has been reborn.
We're back to the basics of God and country
just how our country was formed.

The 'love in' party is over.
Not everyone is so 'nice.'
There are those who want to destroy us
and terror is their device.

9-16-01

Grief

There are stages of grief we must go through
to heal from this horrible crime.
We must weep and pray and be alone -
then someday again - we'll be fine.

We were all in **shock** Tuesday morning.
We could not believe our eyes!
The **realization** of what took place
caught us by surprise.

When this was done, we had to **retreat**
and let it all sink in.
The outrage of this vicious attack
is a horrible, evil sin.

Eventually, there will be a **transition**
when we can weep no more.
Then we'll move to **recovery**
and we'll someday settle the score.

But for now we must be patient.
Healing from grief does take time.
Trust in God and love yourself,
this nation will heal and be fine.

9-16-01

America

America is still a light
in this evil world of ours.
There are good and honest people
who through this shine like stars.

The men aboard the hijacked planes
who gave their lives for others;
They fought the knife carrying terrorists
sacrificing for their 'brothers'.

Three hundred firemen came to rescue
the folks trapped in Tower One.
They never thought of their own lives
and were buried under debris - by the ton.

Yes, good will overcome evil.
It has always been that way.
There is great evil in this world
but God will have His say!

9-18-01

Aftermath

In the aftermath of this horror
twelve 'Dads' from one school are gone.
They were the coaches and support team
and had been for so long.

Now they're gone, but the teams still meet
trying to go on and just play.
But it's difficult without the 'Coach'
who encouraged them - each day.

The 'Dads' are gone - by this senseless attack.
They never could say, "Good Bye."
Their families, devastated by this loss,
- this terrorist attack - from the sky.

Thousands have a story to tell.
What were their dreams and goals?
For this one school, this terrorist attack,
has certainly left a big hole.

9-19-01

Our Response

Our response should have six steps to it
- steps we, as a country, should take.
First we must - **grieve** - for this loss
then heal - for our own sake.

Then be aware that - **no bitterness** -
springs up in our minds and hearts.
It's easy to point fingers
not acknowledging our own part.

We must - **find strength in our God** -
and know that He is there.
He helped the founders of this land.
He's alive and still does care.

We must seek - **divine direction** -
as we deal with this threat.
God can confuse their minds and plots
but give us direction - if we let...

But we must - **respond quickly** -
for that really is the key.
To say, "No more, never again!
We will not let this be!"

We will - **administer justice** -
to protect our own land.
For this is a nation built on rock -
not sinking, shifting sand.

9-16-01

Red, White, and Blue

It's time to be patriotic,
to fly the red, white, and blue.
To stand for what we believe in
regardless what others may do.

This country was founded on freedom
and equality for every man.
But when those freedoms are abused -
we will not let it stand.

The opportunities that this land offers
in the entire world - they are the best.
We all work hard to achieve our goals,
but then we stop and bless.

We bless those who have gone before us
who have died so that we might be
A beacon of light and freedom
standing for the world to see.

9-20-01

Moving On

Americans are strong and tough.
This we must realize.
We will move ahead with our lives
and not be paralyzed.

The American dream is alive and well.
We must all step to the plate.
To protect our nation and freedom for all -
not living in terror is our fate.

We've taken our freedoms for granted
for oh so many years.
Now we must stand together and fight
to eradicate all our fears.

This nation will not be destroyed
by a handful of evil men.
We will regroup and move ahead
- this battle against evil we'll win!

9-22-01

George W.

George W. Bush, we are praying for you
and for your chosen team.
We're thankful you do know your God
and upon Him - you do lean.

We know God has His hand on you
as you lead us through this mess.
We've had a horrible 'wake up call'
but this nation is still the best.

Please know, you do not walk alone
but God's wisdom is with you.
Millions of people are praying for you
in all you say and do.

A three fold cord is not broken -
God - Nation - and Man.
May our great nation turn back to God
so it - like a beacon - can stand!

9-24-01

Heroes

Heroes are made during difficult times.
There are men who rise to the top!
They stand for what is right and good.
They are the cream of the crop!

George W. Bush is one of these men
a leader of strength and courage;
Supporting, encouraging, uniting America
so the people won't be discouraged.

Mayor Giuliani, of New York,
has also stepped to the plate.
He's at ground zero with his teams,
sharing with them - their fate.

These men are just the symbol
of the 'Spirit of the U.S.A.'
Strong, compassionate, courageous,
heroes of our own day.

9-24-01

America Fights Back

Fighting Back

It's a sad day for the
red, white, and blue.
We're under attack but
we know what to do.

The goodness in people
is alive and well,
Helping each other through
this terrorist 'hell.'

It's a fight between
evil forces and good.
But good will win
in the end - as it should.

The evil of terrorists
who have nothing to do,
but destroy and cause havoc
scaring me and you.

But our country is the
best in the world and
we won't let our freedoms
be deterred...

By a handful of evil
and spiteful men,
whose lives portray
the evils of sin.

No! We'll stand firm
and fight - once again.
For freedom and goodness -
not evil and sin.

9-12-01

Forward

One step forward,
then one step back.
This is how 'evil'
does attack.

To keep us in limbo
not knowing our way.
Where we should go -
what we should say.

Confusion is
a terrorist's tool
trying to make us
look like a fool.

But God can confuse
their minds as well -
As they kill the innocent
may they end up in ----.

It is indeed a
'holy war' we fight.
Who will you serve -
darkness or light?

Since September 11th
it's a different world,
and the cells of terrorism
must be deterred.

We must step forward
as a nation so strong -
but we need God's power
so we won't go wrong.

9-24-01

History

"He who doesn't know history is bound to repeat it,"
President Kennedy said long ago.
Being ignorant of our history, we will
repeat the same show.

We hid our head in the sand,
in nineteen thirty nine,
We did not want to get involved
it was Europe's fight at the time.

We didn't want to look at
the problems in Kuwait.
We closed our eyes as our ship at port
was blown apart at the gate.

Over the years, our airplanes
were destroyed in midair.
More bombs, more terror all around
but did we really care?

So now we've repeated history -
by burying our head in the sand.
It took the demise of the World Trade Center
to finally take a stand!

9-26-01

Line in the Sand

We won't run
and we won't hide,
But we will be aware
who's on our side.

September 11th drew the
line in the sand.
Now, all must choose
just where they stand.

For freedom or terror
all must choose.
For one will win
and one will lose.

No more fence-walking
where everyone is nice.
Some want to destroy us
and terror is their device.

We tried for thirty years
to negotiate -
They have schemed and plotted -
planning evil as our fate.

Now it's time, indeed, to take a stand -
and look this evil in the eye.
Three thousand of our very best
did stand - and they did die!

9-26-01

Gone

The gift that God does offer us
is not just 'pie in the sky.'
But the security that He'll be with us -
if we walk or if we fly.

The innocent folks on the airplanes
were just doing their own thing.
When the terrorists attacked, God was there,
and tucked them under His wing.

They did not see the face of death
but rather the face of 'life.'
Christ was there, and drew them to Him
out of that evil and strife.

This is God's promise to all
who carry 'Christian' as their name.
Death will come to all of us
but it will not be all the same.

To know Christ and where you're going
when you leave this planet earth -
Takes the sting out of our exit -
for ahead, is heaven and mirth.

9-27-01

Standing Firm

We will stand firm and we will stand strong,
for You have made us this way.
Fear and terror will not overrun
the magnificent U.S.A.

This country was founded by men of faith
and many trials they did overcome.
To establish a country where freedom prevails
and man can worship God's Son.

But these freedoms extend to other faiths as well,
for we all have the right to choose -
Who and how we worship our God,
being Christians, Muslims, or Jews.

But through our faith, we will stand firm.
Our differences make us unique.
The solid teachings of God's love for man
is now what we all must seek!

9-27-01

Survivors!

In the eyes of those that survived
the horrific terrorist attack
Is a look of fear and horror
but a Spirit that does not lack...

That will to live once again
- to just experience life.
To go back home to be with
their children and their wife.

To engage again in a normal routine
of enjoying life's simple pleasures -
Family, friends, and a faith so strong
these now become real treasures.

Not taking life for granted again
but enjoying each brand new day.
Knowing that in a blink of an eye -
it could all be taken away!

9-27-01

Hindsight

Hindsight is always one hundred percent
judging what's gone on before.
It's easy to judge those who take charge
after we're out of the war.

In times of terror, war, or mayhem
just who does step to the plate?
The brave, the strong, the courageous, step up
those who will guard the gate.

The folks who stand in the midst of battle
making decisions on the spot.
Doing the best that they can do
without complaining a lot.

After the horror is over,
it's easy to look back and say,
"They should have done this - or perhaps that"
But where were you - on that day?

10-01-01

The Survivors

Bless those who have survived this attack
and now will forever be...
Scarred, not only physically but
also emotionally.

The horror of that fateful day
is etched in our minds forever.
We only watched it on T.V. but
we, too, are changed forever.

Bless those that were in the tumbling buildings
running from the burning debris.
Many were caught on fire themselves
- horrid for all to see.

These folks will carry the scars forever,
on their bodies as well as their mind.
A reminder to us that September 11th
has now changed our lives - for all time.

10-03-01

A Choice

Do we live in love or fear?
The two are different indeed.
Love is given by God above,
fear is the 'evil one's' seed.

We have a choice, which way to go
each and every day.
When we choose to walk in love with God
then evil will not have its say.

We are the land of the brave and free
and stand for freedom for all.
Positive thoughts must run through our heads
so we, in turn, won't fall.

This country was founded on freedom and God.
In God we now must trust.
To have His peace within our hearts
at this time is a must!

10-05-01

Being Strong

Life is a mental game
it's true.
Our mind affects
all that we do.

Just what we choose
to think about -
can give us peace
or make us shout!

We have that choice
every day.
What to think
and what to say.

We must stay strong
in these days ahead.
Guarding what we
put in our head.

Fearful thoughts
will lead to gloom.
And soon our life is
full of doom.

So stop that thought
from taking hold -
Cut it off -
be strong - be bold!

Think only on
what's pure and right.
This is how we'll
win this fight!

10-05-01

The People

The Heart of Man

The evil in the hearts of men
always astonishes me.
To kill and destroy what others have done -
how could this ever be?

Terror and killing seem to be rampant -
what do they hope to achieve?
By bombing the landmarks of this world -
then watching the people grieve.

They all speak of goodness, love, and peace
but their actions don't coincide.
They say one thing, then do another.
We can't believe - they lied!

Man's heart is very deceitful
and only by God's great grace -
Can He transform the hearts of men
to make this world a safe place.

10-01-01

All Alone

The shock is over but the effect lingers on
for thousands of American homes.
Those little children who lost their parents
who will forever, come home - alone.

Lisa Beamer, with two young boys,
and pregnant with another;
The boys will never know their father
who gave his life for others.

The widows and children of the firemen
now left behind - all alone.
To try to go on with their lives
running their fatherless homes.

This attack has changed thousands of lives.
They will never be the same.
But, they will go on and be strong
in spite of these terrorist's games.

10-06-01

Children

Having lost my own mother
when I was only eight;
I can relate to the children
who now just sit and wait...

Wait for that door to open
and their dad to come rushing in -
To pick them up with a hug and kiss
then set them down again.

But that will never happen
and the child just wonders - why?
Why did he go and leave me?
Why did he have to die?

Questions adults cannot answer,
much less a child who is young.
The empty spot within their heart
will forever weigh a ton.

10-06-01

It's the People

It's always the people that make a place special
a place where you want to be.
Not the 'big names' that we all know,
but the average American you see.

The firefighters who for day after day
continue - on with their fight.
To find the bodies of loved ones, so dear,
this now has become - their plight.

The policemen who try to protect
what's left of New York City.
They are the nuts and bolts of life
they're not the sitcoms - so witty.

These are the people who 'stand in the gap,'
who are there day after day.
Deep respect I have for them
they are the heroes today!

10-06-01

Tit for Tat

Is life always
tit for tat?
First you hit me,
then I strike back.

All because we
don't agree
On just who our chosen
God should be.

Or how we are to
run our life.
As man and woman
- husband and wife.

The line is drawn
in the sand.
Nations now
must take a stand.

On what they want
for their folks.
Freedom or terror
this is - no joke!

10-08-01

America at War!

I hate to open the morning paper
to see what it does say -
"America is at War!"
is what it said today.

Will we ever live in peace
within ourselves or in this world?
Only if this threat of terror
can somehow be deterred.

To be relaxed and happy
is what we all strive for;
To love our family, friends, and church
this is the American core!

Standing for love and freedom,
in this dark world of ours,
Has always made America
a bright and shining star.

But now, we're at war
and war it must be -
To protect our great freedoms -
for you and for me.

10-08-01

What Can I Do?

The war goes on, and here I sit,
wondering - what can I do?
How can I help or make a difference?
How can I support you?

We are all torn up by our feelings
of anger, grief, and loss.
How can I give support to my friends
as well as to my boss?

The best, and really only thing,
that I can do each day,
Is to lift my friends - and nation up
as I turn to God and pray.

So Lord, my nation and my friends
are in my prayers today.
I ask God to comfort them
and hold them close - this day.

10-09-01

God Bless America!

"God Bless America" is not allowed
according to the A.C.L.U.
Thousands have died because of this saying
protecting the red, white, and blue.

But we are not allowed to mention -
what most Americans believe.
When we now are in a 'holy war'
and three thousand families - grieve.

Just what, today, do we stand for?
What are our core beliefs?
If we stand for nothing - then we will be
a nation of sorrow and grief.

We're now in a major battle
of unseen forces, it's true.
Destroying, corroding, our land from inside
is what they are trying to do.

10-10-01

Moving On

Life does move on, one way or another,
we can only moan so long.
The ache and pain will always remain
never will it be gone.

But how much more of life, I ask,
is really left for me?
It can all be over, in the blink of an eye,
we were all made to see.

So what am I to do
in the days that lie ahead?
How can I be most effective
after all that was done - and said?

I will move ahead
and I will be
A very good friend
to those who need me.

I'll acknowledge the broken, shattered lives
of thousands of Americans this day.
Knowing down in my heart of hearts
we'll forever live a different way.

10-11-01

The Crews

To the pilots and attendants
who continue to fly today;
You are the real heroes
in the war we fight this day.

When your friends and your coworkers
were attacked while on the job,
they had nothing to say and gave their lives
to satisfy this mob.

Our hearts and prayers go out to them
and the families they left behind;
But you knew them as your friends,
you knew their soul and mind.

Hats off to you, for being so brave.
You're the heroes of today.
Your back at work flying
across the U.S.A.

10-15-01

"America" is "United"

In this land of the 'brave and free'
many have stepped to the plate.
The airline crews returning to work
still devastated by their coworkers fate.

Those crews that 'Fly the Friendly Skies'
after what they have been through;
Takes courage and mental discipline
but they do what they must do.

To fly "American" once again
not thinking about the past.
Takes strength of character for these crews
character that does last.

They will stand against this terrorist war
and the values we hold so dear.
The airline crews are our heroes -
they continue to fly without fear.

10-17-01

The Paper

I use to love to get the paper
the first thing in the day.
I could hardly wait to open it
to see what it would say.

But now, it is a different thing
as I go to the curb.
Has the war now escalated?
Has terror been deterred?

I'm a little apprehensive
to see the headlines each day.
The current news of terrorism
is what they usually say.

Perhaps the "I Love Lucy" days
are now a thing of the past.
We find ourselves engaged in war
and wonder - 'How long will it last?'

10-17-01

Standing Up

Martyr or Terrorist

A martyr today and in days of old
died for what he believed in.
He had a conviction and a faith
that was very important to him.

A terrorist also has a strong faith.
But the difference is loud and clear.
He will kill you for what HE believes
and try to fill you with fear.

Both are willing to sacrifice their lives
for what they believe to be true.
The martyr, himself, for his cause
the terrorist, himself - and you!

In this great country, where freedom prevails
you can kill yourself if you like;
But when you kill others, for your beliefs,
then we will have to fight.

10-17-01

Flight #93

"I sought for a man who would
stand in the gap..." God said long ago.
This terrible tragedy of nine - eleven
has raised up several, we know.

Todd Beamer, and others, on Flight 93
became those chosen men.
They fought the terrorists, and gave their lives,
to protect others from evil and sin.

Todd Beamer was a strong Christian.
He stood up for what he believed.
He loved his family, country, and Lord;
now his family is left to grieve.

That grief has now turned to action.
We are now called to take a stand.
We will not forget those who died
who stood up for this great land!

10-18-01

Wake up, Berkeley!

Perhaps those folks in Berkeley
should go live in a Muslim land.
Where women are treated worse than slaves
as they wander around in the sand.

Covered from head to toe -
not ever allowed to speak.
Mutilated as very young girls
so sexually they'll never peak.

Slaves to the men in all areas of life
no rights or opinions have they.
Perhaps the Berkeley feminist
should go live there for a day.

Then they could see what we're fighting for
freedom for a style of life.
Where both men and women have equal rights
as single or as husband and wife.

10-20-01

Lisa

Lisa Beamer, we are proud of you.
You have your priorities straight.
A belief in God, love for your country,
and love for your family - and mate.

One person can make a difference.
You are showing us that with your life.
Standing up and being proactive
as a mother, friend - and wife.

This horrible, horrific, tragedy
has only strengthened your resolve.
You are an example of courage and faith
and a will that will not dissolve.

We will remember those families
and the grief that they do have.
Young children who will now grow up
never knowing their own dad.

We will not forget these folks.
We will support them forever.
As a living memorial to those who died;
a bond that we'll not sever.

10-20-01

His Battle

I will not run
nor will I hide -
when I know the Lord
is on my side.

The evil and hate
in some men's heart -
could paralyze me
so I would not start.

To move forward and
to speak my mind.
Standing up for truths -
truths of all time.

That God is in charge
of this world today.
He's alive - and well
and will have His say.

He is my strength,
my power, and might.
This battle is His
and He will fight.

But I must be willing
to be used by Him,
To help overcome
this evil and sin.

But the battle is His
and we must pray
And follow His leading
every day.

10-21-01

Jehovah or Allah

A luxury we can not afford
are shadow fears today.
Fears that have no substance
but paralyze us each day.

The what if this would happen
if I stepped out this day.
And claimed a holy war
for the Christians and Jews today!

I'm tired of hearing what they believe
"Kill all those infidels.
Murder the women and children too.
Send them all to hell."

By doing this horrible deed,
they are promised a great reward.
Beds strewn with virgins and a great life;
and power so they are not bored.

This is insane - it's time to speak!
Who do you worship this day?
Jehovah who loves or Allah who kills
you must make your choice today.

10-22-01

Peace

Why must we fight a holy war?
Why can't we live in peace?
Why can't man just get along
and have all war - to cease?

Why can't each nation in the world
just run their own affairs?
Why can't the people have free choice
who they will worship - and where?

Why can't we have peace in our hearts;
peace in our own neighborhoods?
Why can't we just all get along
enjoying our life - as we should?

It seems a simple thing to do,
to live in harmony and peace.
But with so many points of view
will killing and war ever cease?

10-22-01

Ache Beyond Language

To ache beyond language
is what we're going through.
In our minds and emotions
we don't know what to do.

We try to go on, with our daily routine,
doing our usual chores.
But our mind races back to events of the past
we are locked behind those doors.

To ache beyond language is grim.
We have all been touched to the core.
Our world has been turned upside down
we can never go back any more.

We will move ahead - somehow.
The ache will someday be less.
This life is full of challenges and pain,
but we will get out of this mess.

10-23-01

"Death to America"

"Death to America" seems to me
to be a wake up call.
The actions - and words - are killing and fear
and they want to kill us all!

Wake up America - there are those who hate us.
They hate the freedoms we possess.
They hate our God and lifestyle
that we've been a nation - blessed.

We now have a great challenge -
fighting an enemy of terror and hate.
How we respond - and what we do -
will determine our nation's fate.

America has fought before
for truth and justice for all.
It's time to wake up America
and stand against this call.

10-23-01

Ache

To ache beyond language
is a poignant way to say,
My life is upside down;
I feel topsy-turvy today.

Life, as I have known it,
has changed - dramatically.
Fear and terror fill the world
on T.V. that's all I see.

I ache for all those families
who have lost loved ones, so dear.
I ache for all the people
who stand up against this fear.

I ache most of all for our country
this great nation of ours.
Our days of innocence are over.
We're now a tarnished star.

10-25-01

Ambushed

Ambushed, captured and killed
as he went along his way.
Abdul Haq was lulled into
Taliban territory today.

Abdul opposed the Taliban -
their horrible, evil ways.
They kill and murder the innocent
if they do stand in their way.

He did speak up for a different view
and was murdered for his stand.
This was like the World Trade Center
but in a far off land.

Permeating around this world
are cells of terror and of hate.
Justice, kindness, and love of life
is not what's on their plate.

10-27-01

War!

From the mountains in Afghanistan
came a weak voice - loud and clear.
"We are in a holy war.
We're right and do not fear."

"We will die for what we believe.
We'll kill those infidels.
Allah is the God we serve
- others we'll send to hell."

Wake up America! Where do you stand
as the infidels in their eyes?
They have killed thousands with their evil way
and more are ready to die.

Where is the passion in the U.S.A.?
What are we willing to die for?
When 'God Bless America' is banned from schools
it's hard to settle the score.

For years, we've turned our back on God.
We'll do it on our own.
Times were good, we had it all,
our hearts were like a stone.

On September 11th, our lives did change,
we had a wake up call.
God, where are you now?
Don't let our nation fall.

The superficial stuff of life
now takes a back seat.
We must dig down within ourselves
and stand firmly - on our feet.

Religious wars, no one likes,
but we all, for something, must stand.
What belief is in your heart -
enough to die for this land?

10-28-01

Front Page

On the front page of the paper
"Twelve Afghans were killed today."
In the bombing of the Taliban
twelve citizens were in the way.

On page four of the same paper -
sixteen Christians were murdered Sunday.
They were gathered together, in Pakistan,
to worship God on their Lord's day.

Why is this the lead story
in the paper today;
When innocent people, gathered to worship,
were murdered yesterday?

In a war there will be casualties
as tragic as that may be.
But the murdering of people, in worship,
is unconscionable to me.

10-30-01

George W. - a Yankee!

George W. Bush, you are the man!
Our nation is proud of you.
You step up and speak for freedom
in all you say and do.

To walk to the mound, in Yankee stadium,
with thousands in the stands...
took courage and great confidence,
you were cheered throughout our land!

We are thankful for a man of character
who will stand up for what he believes.
His God, his country, his fellow man,
as well as with those who grieve.

You are our chosen leader.
Our nation is praying for you.
That you will continue to have
wisdom in all that you do.

11-01-01

Forgive - But Never Forget

"Forgive - but never forget,"
is now what we must do.
The French made up this saying
- after World War II.

They chose to forgive the Germans
for the destruction they did cause.
Killing and destroying
trying to further their own cause.

But the French will never forget -
And we must never too,
For evil men, with evil hearts
won't stop with what they do.

Many Americans have been murdered
over the past thirty years -
Killed by suicide bombers -
as the angry terrorists cheer.

Finally - we got the message,
after so many years.
We will forgive - but not forget -
nor live with hate and fear.

11-03-01

In Memory

One year ago, this very day
we were in shock and disbelief!
The World Trade Center was demolished
much to our horror - and grief.

America is changed forever.
We know this in our heart.
There are those that want to destroy us
and terror is their part.

We must pause and ask ourselves,
'Just what does this all mean?
What will we stand up for
with this enemy that can't be seen?'

They are here, living among us,
smiling and telling us great lies;
Enjoying the goodness of the U.S.A.
while planning our demise.

We will not forget those dear souls
who were all killed on that day.
The cold and calculated manner
these men went about their way.

The Americans on those airplanes
just doing their jobs that day.
They were murdered in cold blood
so the terrorists could have their say.

The lives of the rescue workers
snuffed out in a blink of an eye.
They were only doing their jobs
but so many of them did die.

The thousands of families who lost -
a child or mother or dad;
Will forever be changed for all time,
in their heart, they'll always be sad.

We must forgive this evil act
but we must never forget this day.
We will remember these Americans
who never had a say.

9-11-02

This is a publication of Blue Dot Publishing

Other books written by Sue McCollum

Moving On (before and after cancer)

For additional information please contact:

bluedotpublishing@yahoo.com

or write to:

Blue Dot Publishing
Attention: Sue McCollum
P.O. Box 60725
Palo Alto, CA 94306

All proceeds from the book, *Moving On (before and after cancer),*
will be given to cancer support groups.

All proceeds from the book, *Brave and Free,* will be given to
The Bravest Fund
to benefit the firefighters, police officers,
other rescue personnel, and their families.

★

Order Form

Please send to:

Name: _____

Address: _____

City:_____State:_____Zip: _____

Telephone:_____ e-mail: _____

    Book: <u>Moving On (before and after cancer)</u>

        Book Quantity _____ at $9.95/each _____

        Shipping and Handling $5.00 each _____
        (for one to three books)
        Add $.50 per book after that _____

    Book: <u>BRAVE and FREE</u>

        Book Quantity _____ at $14.95/each _____

        Shipping and Handling $6.00 each _____
        (for one to three books)
        Add $.50 per book after that _____

If shipped in California, add CA sales tax of 8.5% _____

Total: _____

Mail Orders to:	Checks only :
Blue Dot Publishing	Payable to Sue McCollum
P.O. Box 60725	Please allow ten days
Palo Alto, CA 94306 U.S.A.	to process your order